Yellow Sac
S P I D E R S

by Eric Ethan

Gareth Stevens Publishing
A WORLD ALMANAC EDUCATION GROUP COMPANY

Please visit our web site at: www.garethstevens.com
For a free color catalog describing Gareth Stevens Publishing's
list of high-quality books and multimedia programs,
call 1-800-542-2595 (USA) or 1-800-387-3178 (Canada).
Gareth Stevens Publishing's fax: (414) 332-3567.

Library of Congress Cataloging-in-Publication Data

Ethan, Eric.
   Yellow sac spiders / by Eric Ethan.
      p. cm. — (Dangerous spiders—an imagination library series)
   Summary: An introduction to the physical characteristics, behavior, and life cycle of
yellow sac spiders, the most common house spiders in parts of New England and Canada.
   Includes bibliographical references and index.
   ISBN 0-8368-3770-3 (lib. bdg.)
   1. Yellow sac spiders—Juvenile literature. [1. Yellow sac spiders. 2. Spiders.] I. Title.
QL458.42.C4E84   2003
595.4'4—dc21   2003045558

First published in 2004 by
Gareth Stevens Publishing
A World Almanac Education Group Company
330 West Olive Street, Suite 100
Milwaukee, WI 53212 USA

Text: Eric Ethan
Cover design and page layout: Scott M. Krall
Text editor: Susan Ashley
Series editor: Dorothy L. Gibbs
Picture researcher: Todtri Book Publishers

Photo credits: Cover, pp. 5, 11, 15, 21 © Rick Vetter; p. 7 © L. S. Vincent;
p. 19 © Stan Elems/Visuals Unlimited

Every effort has been made to trace the copyright holders for the pictures used in this book.
We apologize in advance for any unintentional omissions and would be pleased to insert the
appropriate acknowledgements in any subsequent edition.

Printed in the United States of America

1 2 3 4 5 6 7 8 9 07 06 05 04 03

**Front cover: The name "yellow sac" is
well suited to this spider, describing both
its color and the kind of web it weaves.**

TABLE OF CONTENTS

Words that appear in the glossary are printed in **boldface** type the first time they occur in the text.

YELLOW SAC SPIDERS

   Although many people in the United States have never heard of them, yellow sacs are one of this country's most dangerous kinds of spiders. Yellow sac spiders are small, but they are more **aggressive** than most other poisonous spiders. In other words, they are more likely to bite if they feel threatened. Not only are yellow sacs willing to bite, but their bites can also be very painful and may take months to heal, often leaving permanent scars.

A yellow sac's bite has never been known to cause death, but, even though this spider might not be deadly, it is definitely dangerous.

WHAT THEY LOOK LIKE

With a name like "yellow sac," you can guess that the color of this spider is yellow. Actually, a yellow sac's color might be any shade of yellow to pale gold. Because the hairs on its body and legs are very short, a yellow sac spider looks smooth.

Like all spiders, yellow sacs have eight legs. Their legs are long and thin, with the two front legs longer than the other six, and with two claws at the end of each leg. The claws help these spiders climb and catch their **prey**.

Including her legs, a fully grown female yellow sac is only about the size of a penny. And males are even smaller than females!

HOW THEY GROW

Baby yellow sac spiders hatch out of tiny white eggs. A female yellow sac lays up to fifty eggs at a time. To protect the eggs, she wraps them in a ball of silk called an egg sac and puts the egg sac in a safe place, where she can guard it. Outdoors, she might hide it under a rock or in a pile of leaves. Indoors, she keeps it in a web, high in the corner of a room.

A few weeks after the female lays her eggs, baby spiders, called spiderlings, come out of the egg sac. A spiderling has a soft body with a hard shell, called a **carapace**, covering it. As the spider's body grows, however, the hard shell does not stretch. When the carapace becomes too small, it breaks open, and the spider crawls out. Then, a new shell begins to harden around the spider's body.

This female yellow sac spider is guarding an egg sac inside her web. The web is outdoors, hidden in a woodpile.

Spiderlings will have several new shells before they are fully grown. Each new shell is the result of a process called **molting**. Unfortunately, molting puts the spider in danger. A spiderling needs its shell to protect its body. While it is waiting for a new shell to harden around it, the spider cannot **defend** itself against other animals.

Yellow sac spiderlings grow quickly. After they are fully grown, however, male yellow sacs usually live only one year. Females live longer so they can lay more eggs. A female yellow sac is able to produce several egg sacs in her lifetime.

This open egg sac shows a small group of eggs, carefully shielded by a female yellow sac spider. The egg sac is attached to the leaf of a plant.

WHERE THEY LIVE

Yellow sac spiders are found all over the United States. Bites have been reported all the way from the west coast to the east coast and from as far south as Georgia to as far north as southern Canada. One possible explanation for why these spiders are so widespread is that they were probably carried from state to state, hidden in crates of fresh fruits and other agricultural products.

In many areas of **New England**, especially Boston, Massachusetts, and in New York City, yellow sacs are common house spiders. In northern areas such as these, the spiders typically move indoors during the colder months of autumn and winter.

Except in cold-weather seasons, most yellow sac spiders live outdoors under rocks, among leaves, or in woodpiles.

THEIR WEBS

The "sac" part of "yellow sac" names the type of web these spiders weave. The web is shaped like a narrow sack or tube. It is open at both ends so, if danger appears at one end, the spider can escape at the other end.

A yellow sac spider spends most of the day hiding in its web. It does not move around very much in the daytime because it is easy to see and might be attacked. In darkness, the yellow sac will leave its web to search for food.

This yellow sac web was woven into a dried leaf. Indoors, a yellow sac spider usually weaves its web at the top of a wall, near the ceiling.

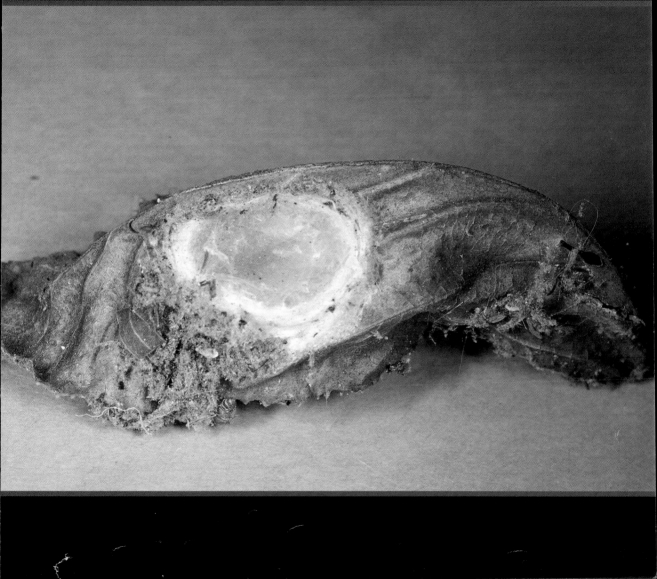

HUNTING FOR FOOD

At night, yellow sac spiders become aggressive hunters. They leave their webs to go on the **prowl** for insects and other spiders. Indoors, they crawl up walls and across ceilings looking for prey. They are good climbers and can move quickly. When they find something to eat, they rush forward and grab it with their long legs.

Yellow sacs use their **fangs** to **inject venom** into their prey. The venom not only kills the victim but also turns the animal's body tissues into a liquid. Spiders cannot chew, so they must **liquify** their prey before they can eat it.

After the yellow sac's venom liquifies this captured housefly's body tissues, the spider will have a good meal.

THEIR BITES

The same venom that kills a yellow sac's prey can cause humans a lot of pain. Yellow sac bites sting! For many people, the stinging feeling will be all they experience. For someone who is more sensitive, however, yellow sac venom might cause soreness and **swelling** around the bite and could also damage body tissues in that area. It can take as long as two months for this kind of bite to completely heal.

The effects of a yellow sac spider's bite are a lot like the effects of a brown recluse or hobo spider's bite. These two dangerous spiders also live in the United States. Before people realized that yellow sac spiders are harmful, they often blamed brown recluse or hobo spiders for yellow sac bites.

A mild reaction to the venom of a yellow sac spider usually amounts to redness and swelling in a wide area around the bite.

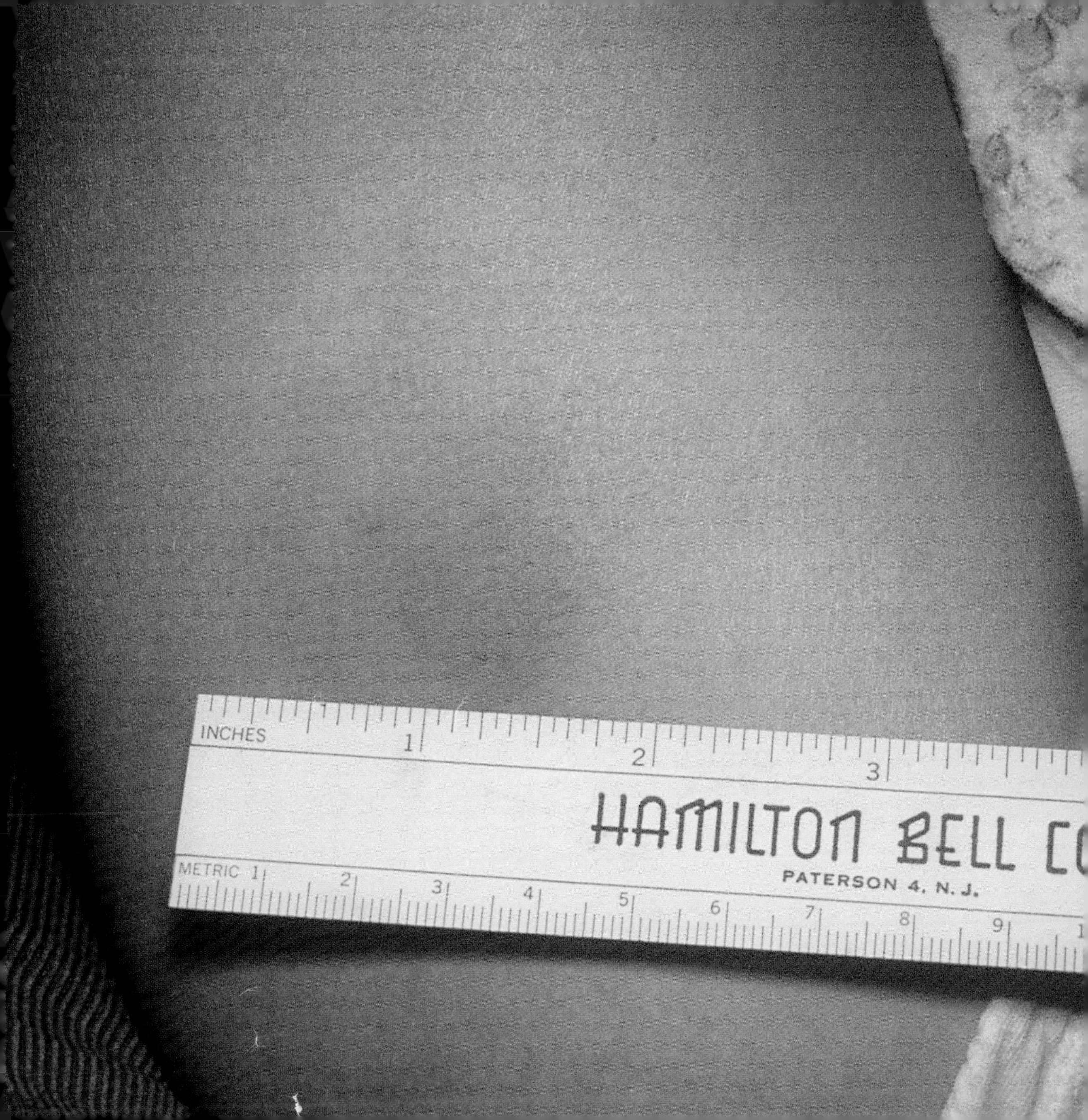

INCHES

1

2

3

HAMILTON BELL CO

PATERSON 4, N.J.

METRIC 1

2

3

4

5

6

7

8

9

THEIR ENEMIES

Just as yellow sac spiders prey on certain kinds of animals to stay alive, other creatures prey on yellow sacs. Birds and many kinds of insects capture and kill yellow sac spiders, especially when the spiders are young. Many yellow sac spiderlings do not live to become adults because they are eaten by insects or other kinds of spiders.

The yellow sac's greatest enemies, however, are human. Because its bite is known to be poisonous, this spider is not a welcome houseguest. To get rid of yellow sac spiders, people destroy their webs and use **insecticides**.

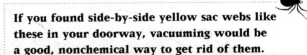

If you found side-by-side yellow sac webs like these in your doorway, vacuuming would be a good, nonchemical way to get rid of them.

MORE TO READ AND VIEW

Books (Nonfiction)
Creepy Spiders. Fearsome, Scary, and Creepy Animals (series). Elaine Landau (Enslow)

A House Spider's Life. Nature Upclose (series). John Himmelman (Children's Press)

I Didn't Know That Spiders Have Fangs. Claire Llewellyn (Millbrook Press)

Life Cycle of a Spider. Ron Fridell and Patricia Walsh (Heinemann Library)

Spider. Killer Creatures (series). David Jefferis and Tony Allan (Raintree/Steck-Vaughn)

The Spider. Life Cycles (series). Sabrina Crewe (Raintree)

Spiders of North America. Animals in Order (series). Ann O. Squire (Franklin Watts)

Spiders Spin Silk. How & Why (series). Elaine Pascoe (Gareth Stevens)

Books (Fiction)
Charlotte's Web. E. B. White (HarperCollins)

Once I Knew a Spider. Jennifer Owings Dewey (Walker & Co.)

The Spider and the Fly. Mary Botham Howitt (Simon & Schuster)

Spider Weaver: A Legend of Kente. Margaret Musgrove and Julia Caims (Scholastic)

Videos (Nonfiction)
Bug City: Spiders & Scorpions. (Schlessinger Media)

Nightmares of Nature: Spider Attack. (National Geographic)

See How They Grow: Insects & Spiders. (Sony Wonder)

WEB SITES

Web sites change frequently, so one or more of the following recommended sites may no longer be available. To find more information about yellow sac spiders, you can also use a good search engine, such as **Yahooligans!** [www.yahooligans.com] or **Google** [www.google.com]. Here are some keywords to help you: *house spiders, poisonous spiders, sac spiders, spider bites, yellow sac.*

**www.biokids.umich.edu/critters/
information/Clubionidae**
Sac spiders are among the species kids can learn about in the *BioKIDS* "Critter Catalog." Although not specifically about yellow sacs and, unfortunately, without photos, this web page has information on sac spiders, in general. Along with a handy question-and-answer format is an equally handy glossary. Click on the little icon of a magnifying glass and a pop-up box with a definition appears! *BioKIDS* "Critter Catalog" has a page about arachnids, too. So don't hesitate to click around.

**www.hurricanepestcontrol.com/
spiders.html**
When you scroll down a little, this web page shows three species of sac spiders, including a yellow sac. The description that follows begins with their bites, followed by details about their feeding habits and environment. Sac spiders share the spotlight on this page with three other "household biters," wolf spiders, black house spiders, and brown recluse spiders (with which yellow sacs are often confused).

**www.ozane.com/profiles/
yellowsacspider.html**
The illustrations of a male and a female yellow sac that begin this page are not as detailed as photographs, but they are certainly better than having no pictures at all. The brief, but clear, information that follows is devoted to yellow sac spiders. It includes information about their family, the Clubionids, and their behaviors. It also tells how to identify yellow sacs — and how to keep them out of the house!

**www.xs4all.nl/~ednieuw/Spiders/
InfoNed/The_spider.html**
This web site is not about yellow sacs. In fact, it's not about sac spiders at all. But it is an exceptional site about spiders. Although the reading level is rather high, it is filled with charts, diagrams, and lots and lots of photos, including some incredible close-ups that picture "the spider" in great detail. Just a click away are one great page after another, telling and showing you about spiders' bodies, their jaws and poison, molting, spiders' legs, silk and webs, a spider's life cycle, and spiders' enemies.

GLOSSARY

You will find these words on the page or pages listed after each definition.
Reading a word in a sentence can help you understand it even better.

aggressive (uh-GRES-iv) — bold and forceful, usually the first to attack or start a fight 4, 16

carapace (KARE-ah-pace) — the hard shell that covers and protects the soft body of an animal and the organs inside it 8

defend (dee-FEND) — to protect or shield from danger or injury 10

fangs (FANGZ) — long, pointed teeth 16

inject (in-JEKT) — to force a liquid into body tissues through a sharp, pointed, needlelike instrument 16

insecticides (in-SEKT-ih-sydz) — chemicals manufactured to kill insects and spiders 20

liquify (LIH-kwih-fye) — to turn a solid into a liquid 16

molting (MOHL-ting) — shedding a covering, such as skin, on the outside of the body 10

New England (nu ING-land) — the name given to the group of six states that are the furthest north in the United States. The New England states are Maine, Vermont, New Hampshire, Massachusetts, Rhode Island, and Connecticut 12

prey (PRAY) — (n) an animal that is killed by another animal for food 6, 16, 18; (v) to hunt and kill for food 20

prowl (PROWL) — (n) a quiet, sneaky search, usually to find prey 16

swelling (SWEL-ing) — a bump or bulge on the skin caused by pressure that is under the skin 18

venom (VEN-um) — poison that an animal produces in its body and passes into a victim by biting or stinging 16, 18

INDEX